Greg's Leg

and

Walk the Plank!

Maverick
Early Readers

'Greg's Leg' and 'Walk the Plank!'
An original concept by Katie Dale
© Katie Dale 2022

Illustrated by Mona Meslier Menuau

Published by MAVERICK ARTS PUBLISHING LTD
Studio 11, City Business Centre, 6 Brighton Road,
Horsham, West Sussex, RH13 5BB
© Maverick Arts Publishing Limited May 2022
+44 (0)1403 256941

A CIP catalogue record for this book is available at the British Library.

ISBN 978-1-84886-875-5

www.maverickbooks.co.uk

This book is rated as: Red Band (Guided Reading)
It follows the requirements for Phase 2/3 phonics.
Most words are decodable, and any non-decodable words are familiar,
supported by the context and/or represented in the artwork.

Greg's Leg

and

Walk the Plank!

By Katie Dale

Illustrated by
Mona Meslier
Menuau

The Letter G

Trace the lower and upper case letter with a finger. Sound out the letter.

*Around,
up,
down,
around*

*Around,
up,
lift,
cross*

Some words to familiarise:

ship   parrot   map

High-frequency words:

has   a   I   is   on   go

the   no   my   to

Tips for Reading 'Greg's Leg'

- Practise the words listed above before reading the story.

- If the reader struggles with any of the other words, ask them to look for sounds they know in the word. Encourage them to sound out the words and help them read the words if necessary.

- After reading the story, ask the reader where Greg went.

Fun Activity

Pretend to be a pirate!

Greg's Leg

Greg has a bad peg leg.

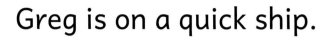

Greg is on a quick ship.

Greg has a red parrot.

The parrot is Pip.

Greg has a big map.

But Greg gets to a peg leg shop.

Greg gets a better peg leg!

The Letter K

Trace the lower and upper case letter with a finger. Sound out the letter.

Down,
lift,
down,
down

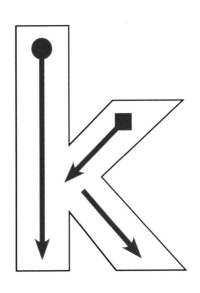

Down,
lift,
down,
down

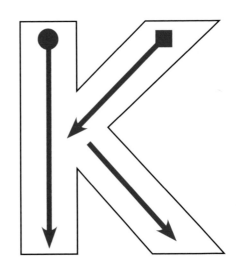

Some words to familiarise:

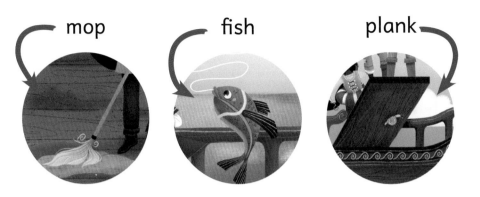

mop   fish   plank

High-frequency words:

the   all   of   you   me   we   go   a

Tips for Reading 'Walk the Plank!'

- Practise the words listed above before reading the story.

- If the reader struggles with any of the other words, ask them to look for sounds they know in the word. Encourage them to sound out the words and help them read the words if necessary.

- After reading the story, ask the reader why the captain told everyone to walk the plank.

Fun Activity

Draw a pirate walking the plank!

Walk the Plank!

Mop the deck, Jan!

Mop, mop, mop!

Now we can all go for a swim!

Book Bands for Guided Reading

The Institute of Education book banding system is a scale of colours that reflects the various levels of reading difficulty. The bands are assigned by taking into account the content, the language style, the layout and phonics. Word, phrase and sentence level work is also taken into consideration.

Maverick Early Readers are a bright, attractive range of books covering the pink to white bands. All of these books have been book banded for guided reading to the industry standard and edited by a leading educational consultant.

To view the whole Maverick Readers scheme, visit our website at www.maverickearlyreaders.com

Or scan the QR code above to view our scheme instantly!